HELLO FROM PLANET EARTH! DWARF PLANETS

Space Science for Kids

Children's Astronomy Books

PROFESSOR GUSTO
EDUCATIONAL & INFORMATIVE BOOKS FOR CHILDREN
(PRE-K / K-12)

Let's talk about Dwarf Planets!

What are the dwarf planets?

Are they really small?

Do they have the same characteristics with other planets in the universe?

How do they differ from the other planets?

Is it a planet or a Satellite?

What is a Dwarf Planet?

According to the International Astronomical Union (IAU), the characteristics of a dwarf planet are the following:

☼ **It orbits around the sun;**

☼ **It has not cleared the objects in the area of its orbit unlike the other planets**

☼ **It is not a satellite**

The significant difference between Dwarf Planets and regular Planets is that planets are more massive than other objects near its orbit and it is gravitationally dominating, while the Dwarf Planets are smaller than a planet and it does not have or dominate its own orbit. They both have their own gravitational attraction.

The Five Officially Recognized Dwarf Planets

There are five recognized dwarf planets in the solar system.

They are Pluto,
Eris, Makemake,
Haumea, and Ceres.

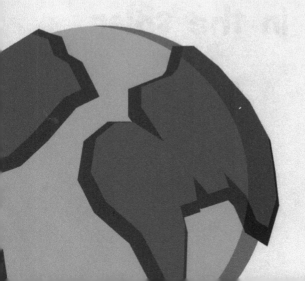

Dwarf Planets

Ceres

Pluto

Kuiper belt   Scattered disk

Haumea   Makemake   Eris

They are similar to other planets in many ways, but they have their distinctive characteristics.

Pluto is the largest, but only second to Eris, in terms of mass.

It was named after the Greek God of the underworld, Hades. It is the second closest dwarf planet to the sun.

Among the five known dwarf planets, Eris has the greatest mass.

It is considered to be the most distant dwarf planet from sun.

It got its name after the Greek goddess of discord and strife.

Makemake is the third largest dwarf planet and large amounts of pure methane ice cover its surface.

It is also considered as the second furthest dwarf planet to the sun. It has an Equatorial Diameter of 1,434 km.

Haumea is the third closest planet from the sun and one of the fastest rotating objects in the universe.

It has an Equatorial Diameter of 1,960 km to 1,518 km. It has an elongated shape.

This dwarf planet is named after the Hawaiian goddess of childbirth and fertility.

Ceres is the fifth known dwarf planet. It is found inside the asteroid belt between planets Mars and Jupiter.

It got its name from the Roman goddess of corn and harvests. The five known dwarf planets, except Ceres, are found in the outer solar system.

It was presumed that there may be as many as **10,000** dwarf planets waiting to be discovered.

Continue to study the stars and outer space.

Maybe you'll discover a dwarf planet next!

CPSIA information can be obtained
at www.ICGtesting.com
Printed in the USA
HW012206240820
146LV00020B/2771